CHI Running

Learn the CHI technique to run
faster, farther, and injury free

By Terence Crawford

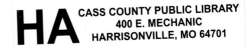

Published in Canada

© Copyright 2015 – Terence Crawford

ISBN-13: 978-1507686423
ISBN-10: 1507686420

Table of Contents

Introduction

Many people avoid running because of the fear of being injured. This is perhaps the reason why most people cannot remember the last time they were seen in the field jogging, let alone running, even when they know that it is good for their health. This book, coupled with my experience as a trainer, provides a solution for this problem.

In this book, I will introduce you to Chi Running, a style of running that aims to reduce the risk of being injured while running. Whether you are a professional looking to achieve prime physical fitness or an average person simply looking to achieve ordinary physical fitness, Chi Running is very useful for you. Keep reading to learn more about the principles of Chi Running and its resulting benefits. You never know, it might be the perfect solution for you.

Chapter 1:
What is Chi Running

Chi Running is a form of running that is meant to reduce the risk of sustaining injuries. Danny Dreyer, an American runner, Tai Chi practitioner, and founder of a North Carolina-based company named Chi Running, developed it in 1999. This style of running uses the basic principles of Tai Chi to help with alignment, proper form, and relaxation for both walking and running. Chi Running also focuses on posture, core, strength, relaxed leg-use, and mindfulness. Generally, the goal is to maintain a straightened back along with a slight forward lean and slightly bent knees. This form of running is founded on four basic skills that we will discuss in turn.

The Four Chi Skills

To better understand Chi Running, we will look at four basic chi-skills. These skills will help you reach any goal in life with greater ease. Although we use them every day, we often do so unconsciously. By consciously practicing chi-skills in your running, you will increase your capacity to focus your mind, sense your body, relax, and maximize the benefits of the most basic of acts – breathing.

Focusing Your Mind

Although it is important for people to develop physical experience first, the mind really does the bulk of the work in Chi Running. Your mind turns off the chatter so it can listen to your body and instructs your muscles to start working or relaxing. Your mind also orchestrates the perfect run by starting out slowly, finding the perfect tempo, and taking in the beauty and chi of your surroundings so that you finish relaxed, empowered, and energized for the day ahead.

When you begin running, your mind must generate willpower to push against the body's natural inertia. Your body is like a stone that will stay at rest until the force of your mind acts upon it.

Body Sensing: High-Speed Access

What is the current state of your body's functions? Body Sensing is the act of feeling what is going on inside your body. When your mind gives a directive to your body, the body will respond with movement, and Body Sensing will tell you the effectiveness of that response. Body Sensing will tell you when you are working too hard or not hard enough.. Body Sensing uses chi to make a link between your body and your mind. Always pay close attention to how your body is responding to input and try detecting even the slightest nuances. For instance, you should feel your posture and feel when your foot hits the ground.. Ask yourself whether you are moving with greater ease or with difficulty and whether you can make any subtle changes in the process.

As you begin running, you must develop Body Sense, and then you will become your own best teacher and coach.

How to Do Body Sensing
Listen Carefully

Pay very close attention to what your body is doing. Practice tuning in to any little nuances, such as how your body is moving and what that feels like. Take note of any sensations in various parts of your body.

Assess the Information

Do your best to discern whether any adjustment you are trying to apply is working or not. If it is, then try to memorize how it feels and how you got there. If it is not, then try to sense what does not feel right. Here are some questions to ask yourself in evaluating your efforts: Do you think your body is moving in the manner in which you wanted it to move? Do you feel more or less discomfort? Do you think that your movement is easier or more difficult?

Adjust Incrementally

Making subtle adjustments is always the best policy. Any abrupt change in how you move your body is an invitation for injury.

Breathing: Tapping Into Your Chi

Breathing is a skill, just like Body Sensing and focusing. It is actually at the core of many Eastern disciplines, such as yoga, tantra, qigong and meditation. Breathing is one way for chi to enter the body. In running, as in all other types of aerobic exercise, the breath is responsible for providing the oxygen that your body needs to fuel your active muscles. Therefore, failing to supply enough oxygen to your muscles means that they will not have the fuel needed for work. There are many reasons why you might become short of breath. These include:

*Low aerobic capacity

*Having tension in your muscles

*Shallow breathing

The greater the efficiency of your body in extracting oxygen from the surroundings and transferring it to your muscles, the higher the likelihood that running will be easier irrespective of your speed.

To belly-breathe, place your hands on your belly button while standing or sitting. Purse your lips in the same manner you would if you were blowing a candle out, and exhale deeply to empty your lungs while pressing the belly button towards the spine. After exhaling as much air as possible, you can relax your belly before inhaling naturally.

Relaxation: The Path of Least Resistance

Tight muscles cannot receive the oxygen they need. The cure is easy – just relax! Do not take yourself too seriously. Drop your shoulders, relax your gluts, smile, and lighten up.

When your muscles are loose and fully relaxed, oxygen that is within the blood can easily enter into the muscle cells for use in various processes.

The three best tools to help you learn to relax are focusing, Body Sensing, and breathing. This is why relaxation completes the list of Chi-Skills. Relaxation is the absence of unnecessary effort. The Chi Running technique allows you to reduce your leg effort, which means you can easily shift emphasis away from your legs so that your body can run more easily. This does not mean that you do not need to use any effort. The point is to eliminate unnecessary effort. This in turn reduces resistance to your forward momentum such that the faster you run, the more you can feel yourself move from your center and the less you need to use your legs. Likewise, the more you gather to your center, the less you use your legs and the faster you run. The cycle works either way.

Relaxing your muscles also comes with other benefits. When you are using only your muscles to move your body, you are doing so with a finite amount of energy stored in your muscles. However, when you use chi energy to move, you are essentially turning your body into a hybrid machine that operates on two kinds of fuel. This is similar to hybrid cars that run on both gas and electricity. The gas engine runs only when necessary (up hills or at higher speeds), and the electric engine takes care of the rest. Additionally, Chi Running technique helps in running on significantly low muscle usage (gas) since your chi energy (electricity) is already doing a huge chunk of the work. The better you get at accessing your chi, the less muscle fuel you will consume.

Simple Exercise

This exercise is intended for when you are not running, so you can get the feel of it and then transfer it into your running when you need to.

Start by sitting on a chair, lying on the floor or standing upright. From there, inhale and try as much as possible to tense all your body muscles at the same time. When you feel you have inhaled and tensed your muscles to some extent, hold this pose as you count to 10, and then release all of the tension that you have been holding in. Repeat this until you are fully confident that you can actually release all of the tight muscles in your body, ensuring that you are very thorough in tensing all of the muscles and relaxing them. Once you have mastered this exercise, try to repeat it when you are running. The more you master the skill, the easier it will be for you to excel in Chi Running.

Can you imagine what our world would be like if the four Chi-Skills—focusing, Body Sensing, breathing, and relaxing—were taught in all life practices? These four areas of human experience are a primary part of our existence, so everyone needs to have them. We do use these skills at different times, but can you imagine having them all engaged at once? The depth of your experience during any activity would be quite different. By practicing these skills in your running, you will eventually find yourself using them in your everyday life thus enriching your experience of self and the world around you.

Chapter 2:
Principles of Chi Running

Chi Running is based on a set of principles that will help you run and train in a more effortless and efficient way. For centuries, Chinese masters studied how nature works and defined these principles in different writings including Tao Te Ching, I Ching, and the practice of T'ai Chi. It is not just the Chinese who have studied these principles. People like Einstein and Newton defined many of them as laws of physics.

The five key principles are:
1. Cotton and Steel: Gather to Your Center
2. Gradual Progress: The Step-by-Step Approach
3. The Pyramid: The Small is Supported by the Large
4. Balance in Motion: Equal Balance & Complementary Balance
5. Non-identification: Moving with Nature

Cotton and Steel

Cotton and Steel is one of the main principles taught in T'ai Chi. It is considered the foundation of all movement in the body. The phrase "Cotton and Steel" describes the feeling that a T'ai Chi practitioner should have while doing the form. When you concentrate chi energy to your center, your legs and arms are as soft as cotton, and hold no tension.

In Chi Running, as in T'ai Chi, all movement in your body originates in your center. It is your power source, acting as the axis around which everything else moves. According to T'ai Chi, your center (also known as dan tien) is located in front of your spine, right below your navel. A series of ligaments, bones, and tendons connect the center to the legs and arms, such that when you move your center, your legs and arms move too. However, in order for your center to do its work efficiently, the rest of your body has to relax and offer no resistance to the movement.

When you run from a place outside your center, it is less powerful because you are doing so from an unbalanced state, and your legs have to work much harder. When you do not run from your center, your running form is not "organized," because your arms, legs, and trunk are moving as three independent entities instead of one harmonious, fluid unit. Without the stability and strength that comes from having a strong center, running is simply moving your arms and legs – going through the motions.

The Step-By-Step Approach

The principle of Gradual Progress says that everything ought to grow incrementally. Whenever growth takes place gradually, each step is usually a foundation to the next step. The principle is also true irrespective of the growth process; it could be a feeling, idea, or life form. An example of the physical plan would be a tree growing from a seed. It starts small and gets larger as the cells multiply, with each growth forming the foundation for further growth.

Another example would be a business start-up. The owner begins a business from an idea. That idea develops into a product or service, which leads to opening the business to the public. The business would start small, and, if the owner did things right, it would grow into a thriving business.

The Gradual Progress principle is widely applied in Chi Running, whether you are doing single runs or a running program. When starting a run, it is important to start slowly and pick up the speed as your body adapts to the movement of running. Just as you would not drive off from a stoplight in fourth gear, you would not start a run or a running program too quickly. Instead, you accelerate through the gears until you reach your cruising speed. Your body is no exception.

For something to become solid, it has to grow step-by-step and move through all of the sequential stages of growth. If you start skipping steps, you are breaking this law, and the consequences can range from fatigue to aches and even injuries. Sixty percent of all running injuries occur because of over-training, which means either too much mileage or too fast of an upgrade in speed. On the emotional level, if you start a program too fast and burn out because of the intensity, you could end up not even wanting to go out and run.

The Pyramid

The Pyramid principle allows you to be very efficient in your movement and economical in your energy consumption. This can translate into being able to run faster or farther because you are not using up your available fuel at a disproportionate rate. It is all about energy conservation. If your smaller muscles are doing the work of a larger muscle, they use up your energy at a higher rate than if the correct muscle is doing the appropriate job. Another place where this principle needs to operate is in your running program.

Your core muscles work your hips and shoulders. Your hips and shoulders, in turn, move your arms and legs. Your arms and legs move your wrists and ankles, and they move your fingers and toes. None of these movements should be out of order, or it will cost you unnecessary energy.

Balanced Motion

In your running, you need to balance your movement and effort. In Chi Running, as in Tai Chi, this balance happens in six directions: left to right, up to down, and front to back. As one part of your body moves forward, its complement moves backwards. As your body leans forward, your stride opens up out the back..

If you run using your legs without bringing in help from the rest of the body, then you are running in an unbalanced state, and your legs will be overworked. If you have a heavy rock to move, it is much easier to have five people spread the workload out. Chi Running is a way to run with all of your body engaged in a unified way, each part doing its proportional share. When all parts are working in harmony, your body moves in a balanced way.

Non-Identification

The Non-Identification principle addresses the theme of moving with nature. Another common phrase to describe this principle is, "go with the flow". When you put your personal preferences aside and align yourself with natural laws, then movements happen as they should. When your ego tries to control the outcome or the process, it throws you out of sync with how events naturally unfold. Non-Identification also implies making friends with injuries and letting them tell you what you are doing wrong. When people tell me that they have had a bad run, it is music to my ears. By simply asking why they considered the run bad, it is easy to pinpoint the specific weakness in their technique and use that to guide them to make the necessary changes. When you start looking at your difficult or challenging runs in this manner, you will not feel the need to call any of them a bad run. Instead, you will be telling your friends that you had a good running lesson.

Chapter 3:
Learning Chi Running
Technique

Most of us are never taught how to run; we just do it. It is important to understand that if you run in a way that hurts your body, you will not be able to continue running very long, and you will also end up injuring yourself. Focusing on form and technique can help you stay injury-free. When you improve your form, you can become a more efficient runner, making it easier to go farther and faster with less effort.

In order to understand the Chi Running technique, it is important to know that Chi Running focuses on leg swing, posture, forward lean and the position of the pelvis. Let us see how these elements affect Chi Running:

Run Tall

When standing straight, your joints are usually in alignment, and your bones support your weight. As you run, you want to maintain this alignment so that your bones remain involved. However, it is common for runners to slump the shoulders or bend at the waist, which then requires the leg muscles to support most of the body weight. Maintaining good posture lessens the amount of work that your legs take on and helps you move efficiently.

Lean Forward

Each day, we have to fight against gravity. Instead of fighting this force, you can harness it.. When you add a slight forward lean to your running, your body falls forward, and you use gravity to propel yourself. Additionally, you keep your body aligned the force of your foot striking the ground. Make sure you do not lean forward so much that you lose control and end up falling instead.

Land on the Mid-Foot

To ensure that your posture is in alignment, and to reduce injuries, make sure that you land with a mid-foot when running. Your goal is to ensure that your foot lands in line with your shoulders and hips.

Run from Your Core

Women tend to complain of hip problems when they run. Core muscles that are not strong enough to keep the pelvis and hips aligned may cause this. To reduce injuries, it is important to keep your pelvis level by engaging your core muscles when running.

Relax

It is common for most runners to tighten their shoulders or muscles as they become tired. However, what you may not realize is this tension and stiffness wastes energy. Each time you feel as though you are tensing up, try to identify the area and relax.

How Hard is it to Change your Running Technique?

It is always possible to change how you run. Nevertheless, it takes time to change how you run. You may need to reduce your running speed so that you can focus on the basics.. It will likely take between one and three months for your muscles to adapt.

Devote at least one run a week to the new technique. Concentrate on the run, and do not talk to a friend or listen to music. Your goal is to focus on how you position your body so that you can make the necessary adjustments. You cannot achieve this when you are talking or listening to music.

Learning Chi Running is like learning how to ride a bike. Therefore, once you learn Chi Running, your muscles remember the movement, and it becomes intuitive.

Chapter 4:
Benefits of Chi Running

Performance Runners

Normally, performance runners are already physically fit. Consequently, they can easily run long distances. Combining this physical ability and the Chi Running principles provides a recipe for success.

Intermediate Runners

The myth that running can easily cause injuries is not true. However, running improperly will cause injuries. Fitness runners can improve their performance greatly when they learn Chi Running as it allows them to relax and conserve energy without compromising on speed. Fitness runners will also train better and more often due to the fewer injuries and reduction in pain.

Novice Runners

One of the barriers that keep people from running is the inability to run more than one or two blocks. Learning the principles of Chi Running will teach you to let your body and gravity do the work. This relaxed technique is does not cause as much strain on the body, allowing you to run further. The more you run, the quicker you will see results.

The Gradual Process Chi Running principle is perfect for a novice runner since it allows you to ease your body into the process and minimizes the risk of injury. It is common for people to give up on running immediately after their first trial, believing that they are not meant to run. However, their use of incorrect form makes them use more energy than necessary. In fact, people are designed to run as long as they use the proper technique.

Injured Runners

Chi running is great for runners with pre-existing injuries because it teaches you to move naturally. Instead of always fighting against your body, you start to cooperate with it, which in turn leads to fewer injuries.

Chapter 5:
Diet for Chi Running

Chi runners need to ensure that they maintain a balanced diet of complex carbohydrates, good fats, lean protein, high fiber, and foods with high water content.

Ensure that you consume complex carbohydrates one or two hours before you run so that you have adequate fuel for your run. Also, ensure that you drink water one or two hours before you run. About one or two hours after your run, eat foods that are high in fiber and water content to replenish what you lost when you sweat. Below are the recommended quantities of the different foods you should be consuming:

First level Foods
The foundation of your Chi Running diet consists of fruits, grains, and vegetables. This first level should account for 60% of your calories with 30% coming from whole grains and the remaining 30% coming from fruits

and vegetables. Ensure that you are consuming complex carbohydrates that provide a steady and long-term source of fuel. Simple carbohydrates do not provide adequate fuel for a run. Oats, bulgur, and brown rice are excellent examples of whole grains you should consume before a run.

Second Level Foods

The next 30% of your caloric intake – the second level of foods – should come from nuts, legumes, seeds and dairy products. Of that 30%, 15% of such intake should come from dairy products, and the remaining 15% should come from seeds, legumes and nuts.

Third Level Foods

The third level of food should consist of meats, including fish, and eggs. This should compose 7% of your caloric intake. Be sure you do not consume too much animal protein since it requires large amounts of energy to digest, thus depleting your chi. If you are a vegetarian, get your protein from plant-based sources like beans, nuts, and nut butters.

Fourth Level Foods

Finally, allow yourself to incorporate simply delicious and indulging foods as 3% of your caloric intake, such as an energy drink or candy.

Below, I have provided a brief overview of foods that will affect your chi.

High Chi Foods
Organic foods
Fresh foods
Freshly prepared foods
Locally grown foods

Low or No Chi Foods
Smoked Foods
Commercially produced condiments
Pickled foods
Foods with preservatives, additives or coloring
Microwaved foods
Most canned foods
Overcooked foods
Fried foods

Chapter 6:
Program Development

The formula for developing a successful Chi Running program is form, distance, and speed—in that specific order. This three-stage method will guarantee that your program will develop safely and gradually. You will not fall prey to the power running mindset of "no pain, no gain" and become injured through overtraining.

You need to work on your form before anything else. Once are able to maintain your form for longer periods, you will be able to build core strength while becoming more relaxed. This component will create the foundation for increased distance, and once you can maintain your form for a longer period of time, increased speed with a lower perceived exertion level becomes attainable. However, if you bypass efficiency and distance and concentrate primarily on speed, you will encounter injuries and a setback in your entire running program.

Conclusion

I began by stating that you that you need not fear running. This book has explained how you can greatly reduce the risks of injury while Chi Running. Remember, the emphasis in Chi Running is on quality and not quantity.

DISCLAIMER AND/OR LEGAL NOTICES: Every effort has been made to accurately represent this book and it's potential. Results vary with every individual, and your results may or may not be different from those depicted. No promises, guarantees or warranties, whether stated or implied, have been made that you will produce any specific result from this book. Your efforts are individual and unique, and may vary from those shown. Your success depends on your efforts, background and motivation.

The material in this publication is provided for educational and informational purposes only and is not intended as medical advice. The information contained in this book should not be used to diagnose or treat any illness, metabolic disorder, disease or health problem. Always consult your physician or health care provider before beginning any nutrition or exercise program. Use of the programs, advice, and information contained in this book is at the sole choice and risk of the reader.

CPSIA information can be obtained at www.ICGtesting.com
Printed in the USA
LVOW10s1816300115

425059LV00010B/299/P